CROSS-ADDICTION:

THE HIDDEN RISK OF

MULTIPLE ADDICTIONS

For many teens, recreational drug use leads to multiple addictions.

THE DRUG ABUSE PREVENTION LIBRARY

CROSS-ADDICTION:

THE HIDDEN RISK OF MULTIPLE ADDICTIONS

Marlys Johnson

THE ROSEN PUBLISHING GROUP, INC.
NEW YORK

Published in 1999 by The Rosen Publishing Group, Inc.
29 East 21st Street, New York, NY 10010

Library of Congress Cataloging-in-Publication Data

Johnson, Marlys C., 1937–
   Cross-addiction / by Marlys Johnson.
      p.   cm. — (The drug abuse prevention library)
   Includes index.
   Summary: Discusses the nature of drug addiction, how addiction to one substance can be transferred to another, and how to recover from addiction.
   ISBN 0-8239-2776-8
   1. drug abuse—juvenile literature. 2. Substance abuse—Juvenile literature. 3. Substance abuse—Prevention—Juvenile literature.
   [1. Drug abuse.] I. Title. II. Series.
HV5809.5.J62   1998
362.29—dc21   98-40731
                                        CIP
                                        AC

Manufactured in the United States of America

Contents

Introduction

*A*nne, like most of her friends, had a lot going on in her life. A junior in high school, she studied hard because she needed good grades to earn a scholarship for college. She was in band and on the swim team, and she had a part-time job. One day Anne mentioned to her friend Ronnie that she was swamped. Ronnie told Anne not to worry; she knew something that could help.

Anne started taking speed occasionally on days when she had swim practice. Then she took it when she wanted to go out after work. Within a few months, she couldn't function without it. Little by little, what started as a quick fix to manage a hectic schedule had become a way to get through the day. Anne's friends noticed she was always on edge. She had difficulty sleeping and was losing weight. Anne had become addicted to speed.

Anne worked hard to get clean. She spent a month in a treatment program, went to teen recovery groups, and followed her counselor's

suggestions. Anne felt that she had her life back
again. She had been off speed for eight months.
It was the end of the school year, and she was
looking forward to the summer.

When Matt asked Anne to the last dance of
the school year, she was thrilled. She had had a
major crush on him all year. Before the dance
there was a party at Matt's house.

"Want a beer?" asked Matt, soon after she
arrived at the party. A big tub of bottled beer sat
on a table on the back porch.

"I'm okay for now," said Anne.

"Okay, I'll be right back," said Matt,
heading for the back door.

One thing Anne had learned in her Narcotics
Anonymous (NA) meetings was to stay away
from all chemicals, including alcohol, while she
was getting clean. It was too risky to use any
drugs. She could relapse, go back to speed, if she
were taking other mind-altering drugs.

The party picked up its pace. More people
arrived and the music was blaring. Matt fin-
ished his beer and was ready for another. He
grabbed two beers out of the barrel.

"Here you go," said Matt, handing one of the
bottles to Anne.

"Oh, no, I ahh . . ." Anne stumbled for words.

"You don't drink beer? No problem. There's
some killer punch in the kitchen," said Matt,
practically shouting.

8

"No, I . . . ," Anne stammered, but Matt was headed for the punch bowl.

Anne struggled with what to do. She was having fun and Matt seemed great. This was their first date and she hoped there'd be more. She didn't want him to think she was a drag.

Alcohol is not my problem, thought Anne. Speed is. Sure, she was supposed to stay away from alcohol and other drugs, but she was clean now. She had been off speed for a while. Everything's cool, thought Anne. She could handle it. When Matt came back and handed her a plastic cup filled with purple punch, she took it.

Anne began seeing a lot of Matt. Every time they went out, they drank. By summer's end, Anne couldn't have a good time without drinking. When band practice started in August, she could barely get up for the early rehearsals. With school starting in two weeks, Anne didn't know how she could keep up her schedule again, what with her job and homework, too. When Anne's friend Ronnie told her about some really good speed making the rounds, Anne said she wanted in on it.

Cross-addiction is a transfer of addictions, the exchange of one harmful dependency for another. Anne had an addiction to amphetamine, or speed, but for several months she had managed to stop taking speed. Then she started to drink alcohol. Soon she needed alcohol to have fun, just as she had needed amphetamine to get all her work done. Anne became hooked on alcohol, and with more demands on her time she began to use amphetamine again, her first addiction.

Saying "I'm in recovery" is only half the battle for a person trying to end an addiction to alcohol or other drugs. Many people recovering from one addiction don't realize that they must also stay away from all other mind-altering drugs to stay sober.

In this book, you will learn how addiction to alcohol and other drugs can lead to cross-addiction. You will also learn what a person must do to recover from cross-addiction and stay drug free.

Scott Weiland (right) of the rock group Stone Temple Pilots, pictured here leaving the police station after being arrested for allegedly possessing heroin, is just one of many famous people who have been caught in the web of addiction.

CHAPTER 1

What Is Drug Addiction?

Many Americans struggle with drug addiction. We hear about our favorite actors or rock stars battling against it. Sometimes we see them win the battle, other times we see them lose that battle. But what does it really mean to be addicted? How does it happen and who is at risk?

Drug addiction is a dependency on mind-altering drugs or alcohol. You may be physically or psychologically addicted to a drug. A physical addiction is when a person's body cannot function without the drug. He or she is primarily using the drug not to get high, but to avoid physically painful withdrawal symptoms and to feel functional. Psychological addiction is when

12 a person mentally craves the high a drug can cause, and believes that he or she cannot live or feel good without it. Some drugs cause both physical and psychological addiction, others just one or the other. Both types of addiction are very hard to break.

Drug Addiction Is a Disease

It was Anthony's first visit to the Alcoholics Anonymous (AA) meeting. When he went into the room, he was nervous. Most of the chairs were filled with people of all ages. They were dressed in everything from business suits to jeans.

Anthony took a seat in the back near the door. He figured he could split unnoticed if he wanted to. From an aisle seat near the middle of the room, a young man about twenty stood up. He walked slowly to the front of the room.

"Hi, everybody. I'm Robert."

"Hi, Robert," everybody replied.

"I'm here tonight because my girlfriend kicked me out. She kicked me out because I got drunk last week. I'm not supposed to drink. I'm an alcoholic. That's not easy for me to say. In fact, that's the first time I've ever said it."

Drug addiction is considered a chronic disease because it affects a person in an ongoing, long-term way. A person does not deal with drug addiction for a few days and then get over it—the addict will be in recovery for the rest of his or her life. That person will have to work very hard to stay clean and win the fight against drug addiction. With treatment, he or she can lead a healthy life.

A person addicted to drugs faces many consequences in his or her life. Drug addiction can lead to many health problems, including sexually transmitted diseases (STDs), such as AIDS. It can lead to crime-related injuries and suicide. This is because people who are addicted will do anything to get drugs. They may steal, lie, or hurt others to maintain their drug supply. They also may hang out with other addicts who are involved in dangerous behavior. Not only will drugs affect a person's health, they may cause problems at school, home, or work. And they affect everybody around the addicted person—family, friends, schoolmates, and others. The longer an addict uses drugs, the worse he or she will get. Without treatment, a person may die.

How Does Addiction Happen?

Drug addiction progresses through various stages of use. When drug use begins, it is

Drug addiction often begins when a person tries a drug recreationally.

usually casual or recreational. A person smokes a marijuana joint a few times a month. Or a person snorts a line of cocaine at a party. But over time, the drug use increases. How long it takes before casual use progresses to addiction is different for everyone. This is because the chemical effect of the drug on the body is different for everyone.

Sometimes a person gets hooked on drugs soon after the first use. Sometimes it takes months, even years, to develop an addiction to drugs. No matter how it develops, no one starts out planning to get addicted.

The body adjusts to a drug and its chemical effect. With prolonged use, it

takes more of the drug for the user to feel | *15*
the same effect. This is called tolerance.
Young people become tolerant of drugs
more quickly because they are growing and
their bodies are changing. Casual use
usually progresses to regular use. Regular
use can lead to drug abuse and addiction.

When a person's drug use has progressed
to the stage of abuse, it is starting to get out
of control. The person spends a lot of time
thinking about using drugs and making
plans to use drugs. He or she may partici-
pate only in activities that revolve around
drugs. Problems arise when life and health
deteriorate and become unmanageable.

Addiction

People who are addicted to drugs or
alcohol are out of control with their drug
use. They might want to stop using but they
can't. No matter how they might plan to
have just a few beers, they will keep drinking, sometimes until they pass out. They
will get high on crack and may even steal
it so that they can keep using.

Drug addiction can cause people to do
things they would not do when sober. They
may lie, steal, or become violent. It doesn't
matter how bad things get, people who are
addicted can't stop using unless they get

16 | help. Their lives eventually become completely unmanageable.

Categories of Drugs

There are four main categories, or kinds, of drugs: depressants, stimulants, hallucinogens, and narcotics. The following is information on all of these drugs and their effects.

Depressants

Depressants slow down the body. When a person takes a depressant, he or she may become drowsy, confused, or uncoordinated. Depressants can also lead to anxiety, restlessness, irregular menstrual periods, sexual impotence, impaired judgment, suicide, and severe withdrawal symptoms. Sleeping pills and tranquilizers such as Valium are depressants. They have many street names, including "downers" and "goofballs."

Alcohol is also a depressant. It goes directly into the bloodstream and affects every system in the body. Along with the many effects that depressants cause on the user, deaths from car crashes are often the result of alcohol use. In fact, alcohol-related crashes are the number-one killer of teens.

Alcohol is the number-one drug choice for both teens and adults and the most widely abused by both. The U.S. Department of Health and Human Services reports

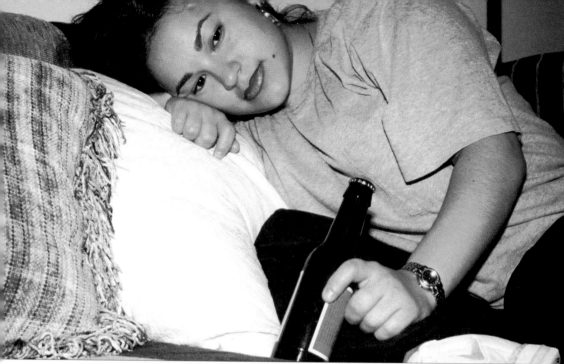

Depressants, such as alcohol, can cause drowsiness.

that one in every eight twelve-year-olds is a binge drinker. According to one study, there were about 3 million teen alcoholics in 1996.

Stimulants

Stimulants have the opposite effect of depressants. They cause the central nervous system and body functions to speed up. Stimulants include amphetamine, meth-amphetamine (crank, ice, crystal meth), cocaine, nicotine, and caffeine.

Cocaine and crack cocaine give the user a temporary sense of power and energy. Crack cocaine causes an extreme high in a few seconds. This is followed by a deep low or depression, edginess, and

The use of hallucinogens can cause trances and an altered view of reality.

cravings that increase with every use. Cocaine and crack cocaine use also can result in violent or erratic behavior; paranoia; psychosis, or loss of touch with reality; and loss of interest in many things, including food and sex.

Hallucinogens

Hallucinogens cause an altered state of mind and hallucinations. LSD, with the street names of "acid," "windowpane," and "blotter," is probably the most commonly used hallucinogen. PCP, or angel dust; mescaline, or peyote; STP, or peace; and MDMA, or Ecstasy, are all hallucinogens.

Physical effects include a trancelike state, euphoria, excitation, insomnia, hallucinations, and convulsions. Hallucinations can cause impaired judgment and coordination, which can result in violent behavior and self-inflicted injury. Hallucinogens can also cause paranoia and flashbacks.

Narcotics

Narcotics include opium, from which heroin and morphine are made. Other narcotics are codeine, Dilaudid, Demerol, Percodan, methadone, and Talwin. All of these drugs, except heroin, have medical uses and may be prescribed by a doctor for pain relief.

Heroin is a highly addictive narcotic. On the street heroin has many names, including "the Big H," "dope," and "smack." Methadone is often prescribed to help with the withdrawal symptoms from heroin addiction.

When a person is using narcotics, he or she can become drowsy, slowed down, euphoric (high), numb, nauseated, or constipated. Besides the strong addiction, the consequences of using narcotics include HIV infection from dirty or shared needles, heart or respiratory problems, mood swings, constipation, tremors, restlessness, coma, and death.

Marijuana and Hash

After alcohol, marijuana is the second most

20 commonly used drug among teens. Commonly called "pot," "grass," or "weed," it is the most widely used illegal drug in the United States. Marijuana is smoked and is sometimes mixed with stronger drugs such as PCP or cocaine.

Smoking marijuana causes problems in thinking, short-term memory, comprehension, and sense of time. It causes coordination problems, which affect the ability to perform certain tasks, such as driving a car. Marijuana also causes sleepiness and hunger. It can cause paranoia, hallucinations, anxiety, and a lack of motivation. Long-term use of marijuana can cause fertility problems in men and women, decreased sex drive, and lung problems.

Hash is a brownish chunk or liquid that is taken orally or smoked. It has similar but stronger effects than marijuana.

Inhalants

Inhalants are common household products such as glue, paint thinner, aerosols, cleaning solutions, and gasoline. Their fumes are sniffed, giving the user an immediate high. Nearly 20 percent of all adolescents report having used inhalants at least once in their lives. Inhalants cause heart palpitations,

Using inhalants can cause your heart to beat irregularly. This can cause chest pain.

dizziness, headaches, and difficulty breathing. One-time use can put you at risk for sudden death, suffocation, hallucinations, severe mood swings, and numbness. Long-term use can cause brain damage, violent behavior, and damage to the central nervous system.

Steroids

Steroids are drugs taken by some athletes and bodybuilders to increase body weight and strength. They also can cause aggressive behavior and acne. They are usually called steroids or "roids." Side effects of steroids include sterility and impotence. Some side effects, such as heart failure and strokes, don't show up for years.

22 | Designer Drugs

Designer drugs are made "underground" in home labs. They are made from certain types of legal drugs specifically for illegal use. They are called analogs of these drugs and are made to be more powerful than the original drugs. Because of this, they can cause brain damage and death.

Designer drugs that act like heroin include MPTP and China White. Designer forms of stimulants include Ecstasy and STP.

Who Can Become Addicted to Drugs?

Anyone can become addicted to drugs. If someone uses drugs regularly, he or she can become physically or psychologically dependent on them.

Some people are considered more at risk to develop an addiction than others. If someone in your family has a history of drug or alcohol addiction or abuses drugs or alcohol, you are more at risk to develop an addiction. A high risk for addiction can be passed from one generation to another.

Some scientists think a high risk for drug addiction is genetic. One study suggests males can inherit a gene for alcoholism from an alcoholic father. Other research suggests you are two to four times more likely to develop some kind of addiction if 23 either of your parents is addicted to drugs. Scientists are continuing to study these issues.

Other experts believe a person learns addictive behavior. People who watch a parent take a drink or pop a pill every time he or she is upset learn that if they are in pain or uncomfortable, alcohol or another drug will make them feel better. But even if a person is at high risk of developing an addiction, he or she can learn to make smart choices and stay away from drugs.

CHAPTER 2

What Is Cross-Addiction?

Susie moved to a new city during her junior year of high school. Although she was getting good grades and had a lot of friends at her old school, she found it difficult to make friends at the new school. It was much bigger and the kids seemed unfriendly.

Before moving, Susie had a drug problem. She was hooked on marijuana. She thought marijuana was a harmless, natural drug, kind of like an herb. It was something she and her friends did together. She never expected to get hooked on it, but she did. As Susie's pot smoking increased, she began to skip classes and her grades dropped. Her parents weren't happy about her failing grades and expressed concern about her lifestyle and the friends she hung out with.

When Susie's family moved, she decided to | **25**
give herself a new start. She quit smoking pot
and was going to clear her head out. She
wanted to try to get her grades back up before
it was too late.

After about a month at the new school,
Susie still felt awkward and uncomfortable.
She started hanging out with kids who
reminded her of her old friends. Not only were
these kids into pot, they also did a lot of other
drugs, like crystal meth, crack cocaine, and
heroin.

Susie's new friends were always doing drugs
around her. It was hard to hang out with them
and not do drugs. Even though she felt like
smoking pot, she didn't want to get started on
it again. She had heard a lot about crystal
meth and thought it might be a kick to try it
once. Susie liked the lift it gave her. She was
able to keep up with her homework and keep
her parents off her back. Soon Susie was using
it every chance she got.

A person recovering from one addiction can become addicted to another chemical substance. That is what happened to Anne in the introduction of this book. She stopped using amphetamine, her drug of choice, and started drinking alcohol. Anne was cross-addicted. She was transferring a dependency

26 from one mind-altering drug to another. A person with a drug addiction can also transfer this dependency to a behavior, such as gambling, sex, exercise, food, or spending money.

Sometimes a person becomes addicted to multiple substances or behaviors. Many experts also refer to this as cross-addiction.

Teens and Cross-Addiction

Teen drug users tend to use whatever drug is most easily available to them. They experiment with different drugs. Because of this, teens are likely to use more than one drug regularly and become poly-drug users. Adult drug users tend to find one or two drugs that they prefer and stay with that drug.

As a teen, you are exploring who you are in the world. You like to try new things and express who you are in new and different ways. You might try different hairstyles or fashions. You might experiment with different types of music to see what you like. Sometimes you try risky new things such as body piercing or experimenting with drugs.

Many teens take drugs to feel that they fit in or to feel more confident. Teens might take drugs to rebel or because of pressures

About 2 percent of sixth-graders have tried marijuana.

In the eighth grade, 55 percent of students have tried alcohol. By the senior year in high school, 91 percent of students have tried alcohol.

By the end of the twelfth grade, 25 percent of students are frequent users of illegal drugs.

Teens who report experimenting with drinking or taking drugs before age fifteen were more likely to abuse alcohol and other drugs than those who experimented after the age of fifteen.

Many teens feel pressure to take drugs to fit in. Some decide that fitting in by taking drugs isn't worth it.

to grow up fast and make adult decisions. They are encouraged by peers and may be influenced by the media to use drugs.

One major reason people become addicted to mind-altering drugs is because drugs make them feel good. They take drugs to avoid uncomfortable feelings such as stress, hurt, loneliness, or boredom. When people stop using alcohol or another drug, they still want to feel good and avoid painful feelings. One way to keep feeling good is to start taking other mind-altering drugs. They learn they can control what they feel by controlling how much and what kind of drugs they are taking.

Taking drugs affects the brain. Taking a hit of crack cocaine, for example, releases a high amount of dopamine, the chemical in the brain that creates a sense of euphoria or pleasure. But eventually the brain needs more drugs to feel the same pleasure. When the drug wears off, it creates depression, anxiety, and agitated behavior. It also causes physical and psychological cravings for the drug.

The longer a person uses drugs, the greater the effect is on the brain. After a person quits taking drugs, it takes a long time for the brain to function normally again. Long-term drug use can permanently affect some areas of the brain, such as memory.

A person may continue to crave drugs for a long time. This can lead to crossaddiction. The person will become convinced that it is okay to take a drug that is not his or her drug of choice.

Cross-Addiction to Behaviors

Anthony had his first sip of beer when he was six years old. It was his mother's beer. She didn't notice; she was drunk herself and passed out on the couch.

Anthony started to take sips regularly. Eventually he began drinking whole cans of beer. By the time he was twelve years old, he had a problem. Anthony was addicted to alcohol.

30 *Anthony got caught with liquor at school. He was put in a teen help group, where he learned about Alcoholics Anonymous. But he never went to an AA meeting.*

About a year later, Anthony started to go to the racetrack with his uncle. He made a little money from baby-sitting and doing errands, and he began to bet on the dog races. He loved to take chances. When he won, it was a real high. Just placing the bets gave him a rush. Sometimes Anthony was ahead and he made a little money. It made him proud to take extra money home to his mom. But most of the time he lost money.

Soon Anthony was borrowing money from friends. Then he took money out of his mother's purse when she wasn't looking. He was starting to shoplift from discount stores and turn the items back in for cash.

Anthony was addicted to gambling. It was a vicious circle. He needed to gamble to feel high. He felt bummed out when he lost money and had to find more money to gamble. The more money he lost, the worse he felt and the more he wanted to drink.

The same kinds of problems or behaviors that led to a drug addiction can lead to a dependency on certain activities. When people stop using a mind-altering drug,

The behavior patterns that result in drug addiction can lead to other addictions, such as exercise addiction.

they may transfer their dependency to these other activities.

A drug addict can also become cross-addicted to unhealthy behaviors. A person addicted to a mind-altering drug can develop an eating disorder such as overeating or bingeing and purging. He or she can become addicted to sex, exercise, gambling, or spending money.

Certain behaviors alter a person's mood because they create powerful and pleasurable chemical reactions in the brain, just like mind-altering drugs. But repeating these behaviors can be harmful. For example, even though exercise is good for you and provides a natural high, too much can cause physical damage.

CHAPTER 3

Why Do People Become Cross-Addicted?

Nikki's favorite thing to do after school was drive home in her car and smoke a joint with the radio tuned to the hard rock station. Every day during her last class, Nikki started to fantasize about her ride home. As soon as the bell rang, she was headed for her car and ready to light up.

Nikki kept her pot in a special tin under her car seat. She always had a few joints rolled and ready to go. Cleaning a new bag of pot and rolling the joints was a ritual Nikki looked forward to.

Nikki usually got her pal Leandra to cruise with her and get high. They had a lot of laughs and understood each other. Whenever they went someplace together, they usually got high.

When Nikki tried to quit smoking pot, she

had a hard time. She couldn't get through the | **33**
last class of the day without fantasizing about
smoking a joint after school. It was a tough
walk to the car every day. If she had a joint
with her, she knew she would smoke it.

Various behavioral patterns come into play when a person is addicted to alcohol or other drugs. One behavior pattern is the way a person uses drugs, or his or her pattern of use. Other behaviors include the defense mechanisms a person uses to defend his or her drug use. These behaviors are often at work when a person becomes cross-addicted.

Pattern of Use
When a teen is addicted to a drug or alcohol, he or she typically uses it in a certain way. This is called the pattern of use. It includes what drug the person uses, how he or she uses the drug, how much he or she uses, and where and when he or she uses the drug.

The drug a teen prefers to use is called his or her drug of choice. An addict has certain ways of using the drug of choice. For example, some teens use drugs with friends or other people. Sometimes they use alone. If someone stops using drugs but continues to hang out with people who use

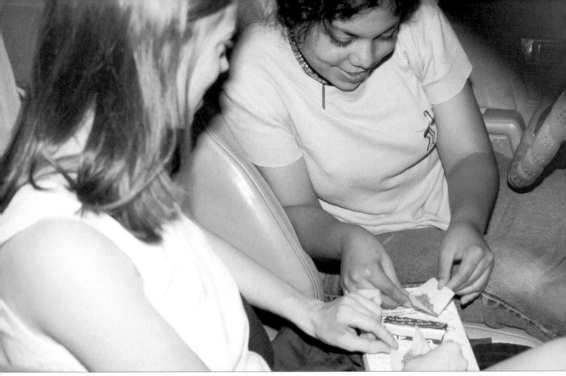

Sometimes being in a place where you've used drugs regularly can cause you to crave the drug again.

drugs, he or she is at risk of using again. Or if he or she does not develop healthier habits, the risk is high that he or she will start using again.

Teens often have favorite places to use drugs. A teen may use while riding in a car, or at parties, or at a friend's house. Maybe the teen uses at home in his or her room. These places become part of the teen's pattern of use. Being at these places can make the person want to use drugs even when he or she is in recovery.

Certain things can trigger drug cravings. For example, just seeing drug paraphernalia such as pipes, needles, or coke spoons can cause a craving. Music, clothes, or

posters associated with using drugs can

remind a person of the drugs and cause a $\quad$
craving. Basically, anything a person has come to associate with his or her drug use is part of the addiction and can trigger the craving for drugs.

Defense Mechanisms

Emotional defense mechanisms allow a drug addict to become convinced that things are okay even when they're not. Addicted people manage to keep using drugs even when their world is falling down around them. Even when they are failing subjects at school or fighting with their parents or stealing or having sex for drugs, they tell themselves things are okay. The addicted person usually does not realize that he or she is using defense mechanisms. Even when the person stops using a drug, the defense mechanisms can keep working in his or her life and lead to cross-addiction.

Denial

One major defense mechanism is denial. People who are in denial about having an addiction do not want to admit they have a problem. They think other people have a problem, but not them. They don't want to believe they can't safely use mind-altering substances. They can't imagine life without

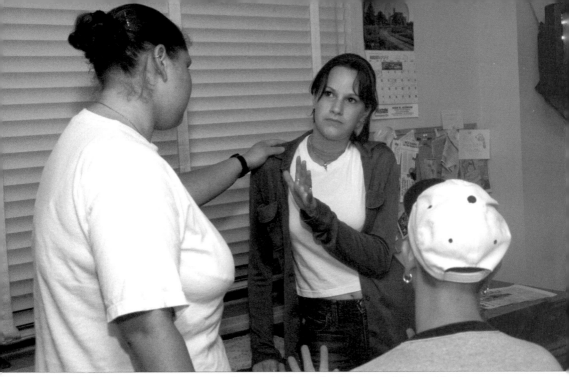

A person may refuse to believe she has a problem with drug addiction even when confronted by friends.

their drug of choice.

The person in denial thinks that making him or her give up the drug of choice would be unfair. He or she sees recovery as being deprived of something.

If you've ever hung out with a person who is in denial about his or her drug problem, you have probably heard statements like:

"I don't really have to use. I can quit anytime."

"I'm a pothead. But drinking's not a problem for me."

"Maybe I can't drink hard liquor, but I can have a beer without any problem."

"It's a party. Why shouldn't I have fun like everybody else? Besides, what's one hit gonna do?"

"How am I supposed to have any fun if I can't have a beer once in a while?"

Rationalization

Another defense mechanism is rationalization. People with an addiction rationalize, or defend, why their drug use is okay. They try to control their drug use by putting rules on how, when, and how much they use. Even if they have stopped using one chemical, they may rationalize the use of other chemicals. They may say things like:

"I only drink beer on weekends."

"I'll only smoke pot. It's natural. I won't use drugs I have to inject."

"I only use when friends give me drugs. I don't have that much of a problem."

"I quit smoking for a month. It was easy. I can always quit again."

Blame

Blame is another way addicted people defend their drug use. They blame other

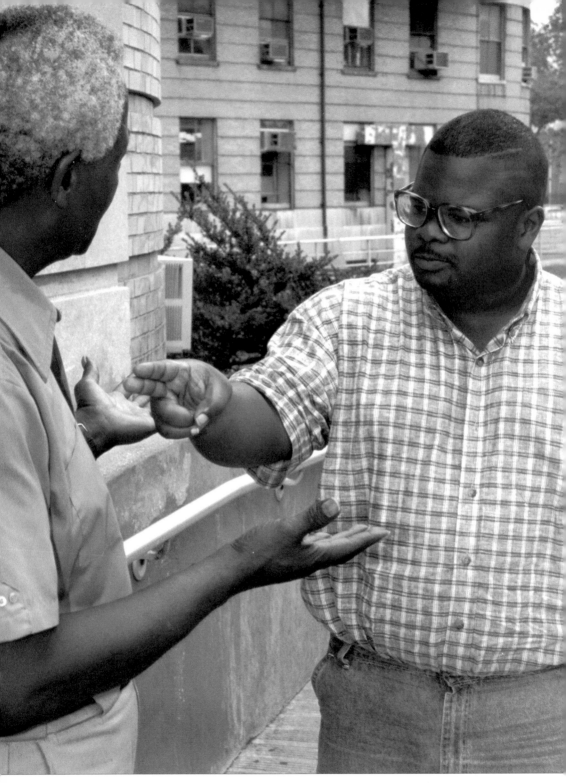

Drug addicts often blame others for their drug problem.

people or situations for their disease. Blame |
puts the responsibility for drug use on others. Then a person does not have to take responsibility for his or her own addiction. If they can convince themselves that other people or circumstances are to blame for making them use, then they can't really be addicted. They may say things like:

"I wouldn't be addicted if my parents understood me."

"If I didn't have so much homework, I wouldn't have to smoke pot to relax."

"I wouldn't have to drink if my coach wasn't so hard on me."

Minimization

People with a drug problem make their drug use seem like less of a problem than it really is. This is the defense mechanism called minimization. They may say:

"My using doesn't really hurt anyone."

"I don't spend much money on drugs."

"I only have a couple of drinks at a time. I can't really be addicted."

40 A person use any of these defense mechanisms, and it can lead to a second addiction.

Relapse

Relapse is when a person who has been in recovery starts using drugs again. He or she may go back to his or her drug of choice or start using a different drug. This can be very devastating to the person in recovery. He or she may feel like a failure and believe recovering from drugs is hopeless. But this is not true.

A person who is trying to recover from a drug addiction often relapses several times. Experts now think this is part of the disease of addiction. The person can continue to crave drugs for a long time after beginning the recovery process. This makes him or her vulnerable to relapse. But there are ways to learn to deal with cravings and to recover from drug dependency and cross-addiction.

CHAPTER 4

Recovering from Cross-Addiction

*W*hen you are cross-addicted, the hardest thing to do is admit that you have a problem. Most people don't like to admit that they have problems of any kind. Part of being a teen is learning to take care of yourself and to solve your own problems. When you have a drug problem, you can't solve it alone. Before you can get better, you have to admit you can't fix the drug problem by yourself.

Another reason people don't like to admit they have a problem is the shame and guilt they feel about using drugs. In our culture, there is a stigma attached to drug addiction. This means some people look at those with an addiction as weak and undesirable. They think of all drug-addicted people as bums or gang members. They don't realize that

41

Support groups are a good way to get help recovering from a drug addiction.

anybody can become addicted to drugs and need help to recover.

Getting Help

There are many ways to get help for cross-addiction. Self-help support groups such as Alcoholics Anonymous and Narcotics Anonymous are important because they offer meetings where people who are in recovery share what it's really like to have an addiction. They know how hard it is to stay drug free and how important it is to get help for addiction.

Treatment programs are essential for recovery. These programs, held in a drug-free atmosphere, help you learn the skills you need to stay off drugs. Counselors, ministers, and doctors also can help you learn about recovery. Or they can suggest someone you can talk to who understands addiction.

Understanding Your Pattern of Using

To recover from cross-addiction, you must understand your pattern of using drugs. This means you must look at the way you have used drugs so that you can recognize danger signs or triggers. Triggers can cause you to relapse and go back to using drugs. Or they can lead to another addiction. You must look at the people, places, and things that were part of your addiction.

To recover from cross-addiction, a person must generally avoid the people he or she once used drugs with. Although you don't plan to use again, hanging around people who use can trigger your craving for drugs. It is not easy to leave behind old friends or make new ones. But being with people who are drug free is a vital part of recovering from cross-addiction.

It's also important to avoid the places where you used to do drugs. It is not always possible to avoid certain places. If you used in your room, for example, you can't stop going there. But you can limit your time there and plan interesting, healthy activities that are not related to drugs when you are in your room.

It is difficult for a recovering drug addict to be around drugs or people who use them.

Staying off drugs also means getting rid of the things you associate with your drug use. Drug paraphernalia, posters, clothes, and music that were part of your drug use can trigger cravings.

Most important, to recover from cross-addiction, you can't have drugs around anywhere. Some people keep a joint or a hit of speed around, just in case. They try to test their willpower by doing this. But having drugs within easy reach will most likely lead to a relapse.

When you have a craving for drugs, you can learn to call a friend who is also in recovery, or walk around the block until your head clears and the craving passes. Support groups can give you other ideas and provide a sense of community and caring, which is also important in the recovery process.

Confronting Defense Mechanisms
Learning to confront your defense mechanisms is another important tool to recovery and to leading a drug-free life. Narcotics Anonymous and Alcoholics Anonymous groups can help you learn to recognize and deal with your defense mechanisms. You can also talk to a counselor or psychologist who has experience working with addiction problems.

Structuring Your Time
Having time with nothing to do can bring up the pain and problems you were trying to avoid by using drugs and can start the old thinking patterns again. It can be easy to quickly convince yourself to drive down the block where your dealer hangs out, or to go to the house of a friend who uses. Until you have fully mastered how to deal in a healthy way with your problems, structuring your time with activities that you enjoy can help you stay drug free.

This can mean getting a part-time job, planning time with sober friends, joining a church group, or going to support group meetings. It may take time to find the right

46 | activities for you. Many people find sports, writing, painting, playing music, or just talking to be effective and fulfilling.

Recovering from Addictive Behaviors

If a person is addicted to a certain behavior, he or she can sometimes recover from that behavior by stopping the activity. A person addicted to gambling, for example, can stop going to the places where he or she gambles.

But other activities are necessary in life. We all have to eat and spend money. Exercise and sex are healthy and natural parts of life. If you are cross-addicted to these behaviors, the challenge is to learn ways to limit them to healthy patterns.

Support groups can teach you the skills you need to limit and control addictive behaviors. Gamblers Anonymous and Overeaters Anonymous are two such groups that help people with these types of addictions.

Moving Toward Sobriety

As a teen, you are growing emotionally, mentally, spiritually, and physically. You are also developing your independence. You are learning social skills, such as making friends and building strong relationships. You are planning for your future.

When you become addicted to drugs, you stop doing many of these things. In

A part of recovery is rebuilding social relationships.

recovering from cross-addiction, you may need to focus on rebuilding social skills and learning constructive life skills as part of becoming a healthy adult with a full, productive life.

In recovery, you also learn how to deal with your emotions. Many of these feelings can be very painful, especially memories of abuse or loss. Some experts think stress is a reason many people start to abuse drugs and become addicted to them. When you are in recovery, you learn healthy ways to handle stress and other feelings. These may include journaling and talking to friends and family to openly express your needs and feelings. Avoiding your feelings can lead to relapse.

48   In recovery, you will learn to watch for when you are hungry, angry, lonely, or tired. Any of these feelings can lead to craving drugs or developing addictive behaviors.

Attending Support Groups

Attending support groups like Alcoholics Anonymous or Narcotics Anonymous is an important part of the recovery process because members know what it's like to suffer from addiction. Meetings are free and are usually held weekly. People talk openly about their feelings and share ways to stay drug free.

Many support groups are listed in the telephone directory. Some groups have 800 numbers you can call to find a group in your area. Look in the Where to Go for Help section in the back of this book for more resources.

CHAPTER 5

Staying Drug Free

*T*he teen years can be difficult. There are many pressures in your life, and it's not always easy to stay drug free. But you can choose positive influences and productive activities that will lead to a healthy life.

Productive Activities

There are many ways to find enjoyment and meaning and to feel good without putting your health at risk. Physical exercise releases endorphins, the body's natural painkillers, so you automatically feel good. Try activities like skateboarding, dancing, weight lifting, bike riding, and swimming. Most types of physical activity that increase your heart rate and breathing for an extended period of time can create a natural high. But remember, it's

Trying a new sport, such as skateboarding, can give you some of the fun you may be looking for.

important not to take exercise to an extreme. Compulsive exercise, or exercise addiction, can hurt more than help you.

There are safe ways to take risks and experiment in your life. Rock climbing, traveling to new places, and learning a new craft or skill are ways to find adventure and thrills. These activities can be exciting and challenging without creating the lows and shameful feelings that come from drug use.

Entertain Yourself

You can expand your life with activities that both entertain and educate. Going to concerts, listening to music, going to museums or to plays are ways to experience pleasure and learn about music, history, or the theater. Reading a good book, taking singing or acting lessons, learning to build things, or learning a foreign language can expand your mind in new ways. They also provide fulfillment, which many drug-addicted people say is missing from their lives.

Feel Good About Yourself

Feeling good about yourself is a sure way to stay drug free. When you feel good about yourself, you don't want to take chances in your life that can cause long-lasting damage. In the long term, drug use does not make

Volunteering in your community can help you create friendships and connections with other people.

you feel good about yourself. After the drug high come depression, shame, guilt, and possible long-term health problems.

Volunteer activities can be rewarding and make you feel good about yourself. Become a mentor to someone younger than you. Volunteer at a homeless shelter. Help build a house for the poor. Baby-sit, or visit an elderly person. Help clean up your neighborhood. Getting involved in your community makes you feel connected to other people and to life.

Learning new skills makes you feel good about yourself. So does doing well at school or work, or in sports or music. They all provide a sense of accomplishment and pride.

Feeling good about yourself includes

feeling good about your body. Getting
physically fit, eating healthy foods, and experimenting with clothes and hair are all ways to feel good about the way you look. When you feel healthy, you won't want to put harmful chemicals into your body.

If you find yourself feeling depressed for a long period of time, seek help from a professional such as a doctor, counselor, or therapist. Everybody feels down once in a while. Teens experience many different feelings. Physical and emotional changes can make you feel awkward and unsure of yourself, and feeling depressed can lead to drug use. Talk to a trusted adult about your feelings. Ask your doctor or school guidance counselor for advice. They can connect you to services to help with depression and other problems.

Managing Stress

As a teen, you experience many pressures in your life. Your parents have certain expectations of you. School and teachers may place high standards on your performance. Coaches, bosses, boyfriends or girlfriends, and peers can have expectations of you too.

You are also expected to figure out what you want to do with your life at a time when you have tons of homework, may be involved

One way to reduce stress in your life is to set realistic goals for yourself. Try to focus on one thing at a time.

in extracurricular activities, or are holding a part-time job. Often you have major responsibilities at home as well.

Like other skills, managing stress is a skill that you can learn. Setting limits on how much you can do in a day or week is a start. Telling people how you feel about their expectations of you, relaxing and having downtime, and getting enough exercise are all healthy ways to manage stress. Counseling and therapy can also help.

Setting Goals

If you think about and set specific goals in your life, you are more likely to achieve them. Short-term goals, like what you want to accomplish this week, can help you focus on what you want to do. Long-term goals for the school year or even five years from now help you see what steps you need to take to achieve them. Having manageable, realistic goals is another good way to stay drug free.

Choose Positive People

Hanging out with positive people is important for many reasons. Having role models who are positive and drug free can help show you the way to achieve sobriety and healthy living. Friends who are not using drugs are the best kind of friends to have. Good friends encourage you to do well and to feel good about yourself. If you are around people who are doing positive, productive things, it helps you stay positive, productive, and—best of all—drug free.

There are many ways to stay drug free. Find the ways that work best for you. Recognizing that you are suffering from an addiction is an important first step. When you make the decision to fight an addiction, you are making the decision to change your life for the better. It won't be easy, but it will be one of the most rewarding things you ever do for yourself.

Glossary

AIDS (acquired immunodeficiency syndrome) Disease caused by the HIV virus and transmitted by blood and other bodily fluids; usually fatal.

amphetamine Substance used as a stimulant of the central nervous system.

analog Chemical that is similar to another in structure but different in composition, and may be more powerful.

chronic Of long duration or frequent recurrence.

cross-addiction Condition of suffering from more than one addiction at a time or replacing one addiction with another.

defense mechanism Mental process of defending one's behavior.

depressant Substance that slows down bodily and mental activities.

dopamine Chemical acting in the brain to help regulate movement and emotion.

hallucinogen Substance that produces perception of objects or sounds not based in reality.

impotence Inability of a male to attain or sustain an erection.

menstrual period Monthly discharge of blood and tissue debris from the uterus.

sexually transmitted disease (STD) One of several diseases transmitted by sexual activity.

sterility Inability to reproduce.

stigma A mark of disgrace or shame on one's reputation.

stimulant Substance that speeds up the central nervous system and bodily functions.

tolerance The body's adjustment to a drug to the point that more of the drug is required to achieve the same effect.

withdrawal symptom Painful mental or physical reaction to stopping use of a drug.

Where to Go for Help

Al-Anon/Alateen Family Group Headquarters
1600 Corporate Landing Parkway
Virginia Beach, VA 23454
(888) 4AL-ANON (U.S. and Canada)
Web site: http://www.al-anon.alateen.org

Alcoholics Anonymous (AA) World Services
475 Riverside Drive
New York, NY 10115
(212) 870-3400
Web site: http://www.aa.org

Children of Alcoholics Foundation, Inc.
Box 4185, Grand Central Station
New York, NY 10115
(800) 359-2623
Web site: http://www.drughelp.org

Co-Anon Family Groups
P.O. Box 64742-66
Los Angeles, CA 90064

(310) 859-2206
Web site: http://www.co-anon.org

Cocaine Anonymous (CA)
World Service Office
P.O. Box 2000
Los Angeles, CA 90049
(800) 347-8998
Web site: http://www.ca.org

Co-Dependents Anonymous / CoDA - Teen
P.O. Box 33577
Phoenix, AZ 85067-3577
(602) 277-7991
Web site: http://www.ourcoda.org

Families Anonymous, Inc.
P.O. Box 3475
Culver City, CA 90231-3475
(800) 736-9805
Web site:
   http://home.earthlink.net/~famanon/index.html

Nar-Anon Family Groups
P.O. Box 2562
Palos Verdes Peninsula, CA 90274
(310) 547-5800

Narcotics Anonymous (NA)
World Service Office
P.O. Box 9999
Van Nuys, CA 91409
(818) 773-9999
Web site: http://www.na.org

60 | **National Association for Children of Alcoholics**
11426 Rockville Pike, Suite 100
Rockville, MD 20852
(888) 554-2627
Web site: http://www.health.org/nacoa

National Clearinghouse for Alcohol and Drug Information
P.O. Box 2345
Rockville, MD 20847-2345
(800) 729-6686
Web site: http://www.health.org

National Council on Alcoholism and Drug Dependence, Inc.
12 West 21st Street, 7th Floor
New York, NY 10010
(800) 622-2255
Web site: http://www.ncadd.org

National Families in Action
2957 Clairmont Road, Suite 150
Atlanta, GA 30329
(404) 248-9676
Web site: http://www.emory.edu/NFIA/

In Canada

Addictions Foundation of Manitoba
1031 Portage Avenue
Winnipeg, MB R3G 0R8
(204) 944-6200
Web site: http://www.afm.mb.ca

Alcoholics Anonymous Family Groups
P. O. Box 6433, Station J
Ottawa, ON M4P 1K5
(613) 722-1830
World Directory Meeting Line: (800) 443-4525

Kids Help
439 University Avenue, Suite 300
Toronto, ON M5G 1Y8
(800) 668-6868
Web site: http://kidshelp.sympatico.ca/index.html

Hotline

**Center for Substance Abuse Treatment
  Information and Treatment Referral**
(800) 662-4357

Web Sites

Moyers on Addiction: Close to Home
http://www.pbs.org/wnet/closetohome

Recovery Online
http://www.netwizards.net/recovery/index/html

For Further Reading

Claypool-Miner, Jane. *Alcohol and You.* New York: Franklin Watts, 1997.

———. *Drugs and Fitting In.* New York: Rosen Publishing Group, 1998.

Glass, George. *Narcotics: Dangerous Painkillers.* New York: Rosen Publishing Group, 1998.

Heuer, Marti. *Happy Daze.* Denver: MAC Publishing, 1986.

Schaefer, Dick. *Choices and Consequences: What to Do When a Teenager Uses Alcohol/Drugs.* Minneapolis: Johnson Institute Books, 1987.

Schwartz, Linda. *Drug Questions and Answers.* Santa Barbara: The Learning Works, 1991.

Smith-McLaughlin, Miriam, and Sandra Peyser-Hazouri. *Addiction: The High That Brings You Down.* Springfield, NJ: Enslow Publishers, Inc., 1997.

Somdahl, Gary L., and Edward Maloney. *Drugs and Kids: How Parents Can Keep Them Apart.* Salem, OR: Dimi Press, 1996.

Index

About the Author

Marlys Johnson, M.Ed., LPC, worked as a children's and family therapist for seven years. For four years, she worked directly with the chemically dependent. She was a children's therapist at a residential treatment program for women at McCambridge Center in Columbia, Missouri. Prior to this, she worked as a teacher and behavioral consultant. Currently, Ms. Johnson works as a journalist and freelance writer. She has written over 50 articles on various topics, including health and business, and profiles of people of interest.

Photo Credits

p. 2 by Seth Dinnerman; p. 10 © AP/Wide World Photos; pp. 14, 17, 21, 28, 31, 34, 36, 38, 44, 47, 50, 52, 54 by Brian Silak; pp. 18, 42 by Ira Fox.